Philosophy Adventure™ Student Workbook

Philosophy Adventure™ Student Workbook

a Home School Adventure Co. Curriculum

Enjoy the journey!

Philosophy Adventure™—Pre-Socratics: Student Workbook

Learn how to **WRITE SKILLFULLY,**
THINK CRITICALLY, and
SPEAK ARTICULATELY
as you explore the history of philosophy
and the world of ideas.™

Copyright 2013 Stacy Farrell
978-1-937494-05-6 — Print Edition

All rights reserved. No part of this publication may otherwise be published, reproduced, stored in a retrieval system, or transmitted or copied in any form or by any means now known or hereafter developed, whether electronic, mechanical, or otherwise, without prior written permission of the publisher.

Illegal use, copying, publication, transfer or distribution is considered copyright infringement according to Sections 107 and 108 and other relevant portions of the United States Copyright Act.

Unless otherwise indicated, all Scripture quotations are from The Holy Bible, English Standard Version® (ESV®), copyright © 2001 by Crossway, a publishing ministry of Good News Publishers. Used by permission. All rights reserved.

Cover Design: Stacy Farrell
Cover Art: Commonly known as "School of Athens" fresco painted by the Great Renaissance master Raphael

Published and Printed by
Revelation Press
a division of
Home School Adventure Co.®
P. O. Box 162
South Elgin, IL 60177

homeschooladventure.com

DEDICATED TO JESUS,
THE ANSWER

CONTENTS

Notebook Pages, Maps, & Creative freewritings   ix

    Thales   1

    Pythagoras   7

    Xenophanes   13

    Heraclitus   19

    Parmenides   25

    Empedocles   31

    Protagoras   37

    Democritus   43

Write ✝ Think ✝ Speak Journal   49

    Thales   51

    Pythagoras   55

    Xenophanes   61

    Heraclitus   67

PARMENIDES	71
EMPEDOCLES	75
PROTAGORAS	79
DEMOCRITUS	83
CHECKLISTS	**105**
START	107
SUBSTANCE	109
STRUCTURE	111
STYLE	113
POLISH	115
PEER CRITIQUE	117
EVALUATION	119
GLOSSARY	**121**

NOTEBOOK PAGES, MAPS, & CREATIVE FREEWRITINGS

MEET THE PHILOSOPHER
THALES

Title(s):

Famous Quote:

Name Thales' birthplace and three destinations to which he is believed to have traveled.

What made Thales different from other influential thinkers before him?

How do we know what Thales believed?

What did Thales identify as the arche (essential substance of life), and why?

LESSON 1

HIS STORY UNFOLDS

In the beginning of Western philosophy, what three disciplines were intermingled?

What were some of Thales' achievements?

What foundational belief held by Thales sharply conflicts with a biblical worldview?

According to Diogenes Laertius, how did Thales die?

THALES

EXPLORE HIS WORLD

THALES

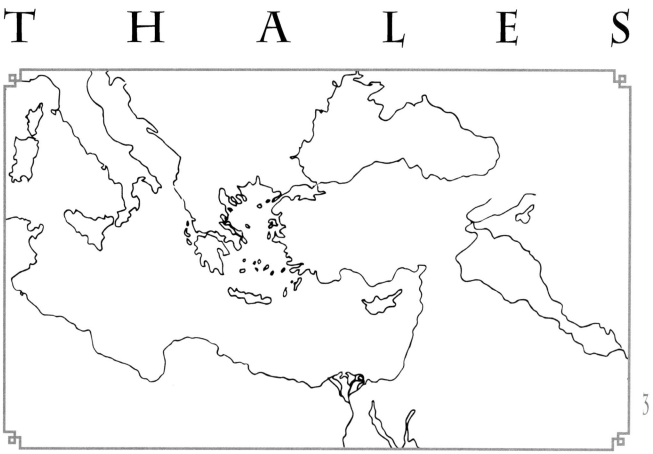

IN THE SPACE PROVIDED BELOW,
LABEL EACH LOCATION ON THE MAP AND RECORD FACTS FROM THE TEXT.

MILETUS	
HAYLS RIVER	
EGYPT	
BABYLON	
LYDIA	
DELPHI	

LESSON 1

CREATIVITY & CRITICAL THINKING UNLEASHED

THALES

WRITING TIPS

It is far easier to be engaging in your writing when you choose a subject about which you are passionate.

Like most skills, good writing is developed through practice. It is similar to playing scales on an instrument. If you do not do so already, start a journal and commit to writing in it at least five minutes every day.

To further develop your writing skills, surprisingly, it can be better to invest the entire quarter writing and rewriting one finely crafted paper than to write several unpolished papers and, in the process, establish the habit of prolific yet half-hearted writing.

Give yourself permission to write really "terrible" first drafts. (We will talk more about the concept of the "terrible" first draft later.) Then, once you have some raw material, work and rework your piece until it communicates your message with clarity and elegance.

THALES, THE STAR GAZER

Your Setting: You are carrying your water pitcher to the well to draw water.

The Action: You see this funny old man leaning into the well. Suddenly he leans too far, and you see him tumble in!

Your Assignment: Describe the scene and tell what happens.

Background: Is there anything you would like to say to set up the scene?

The Dialogue: Do you speak with Thales? What does he say?

Your Senses:

- What do you see?
- What do you hear?
- What do you smell?
- What temperature and textures do you encounter?
- Do you taste the water?

Set the timer for fifteen minutes, use the back of this page, and *write!*

LESSON 1

CREATIVITY & CRITICAL THINKING UNLEASHED

6

THALES

MEET THE PHILOSOPHER
PYTHAGORAS

Title(s):

Famous Quote:

Name Pythagoras' birthplace and three destinations to which he is believed to have traveled.

What ancient greek philosopher did Pythagoras supposedly meet, and what advice did he give to Pythagoras?

Did Pythagoras discover the Pythagorean Theorem? If not, who did?

What is the name of Pythagoras' homeland and what is one explanation for why he left it?

LESSON 2

ᏣᎳ HIS STORY UNFOLDS

What are some of the requirements he placed on his followers?

What did Pythagoras supposedly have such a strong adversion to that ultimately contribted to his death. Summarize the story.

What foundational belief held by Pythagoras sharply conflicts with a biblical worldview?

Name at least two legends about Pythagoras that spread in the first and second centuries. Provide a possible explanation for why they arose.

PYTHAGORAS

EXPLORE HIS WORLD
PYTHAGORAS

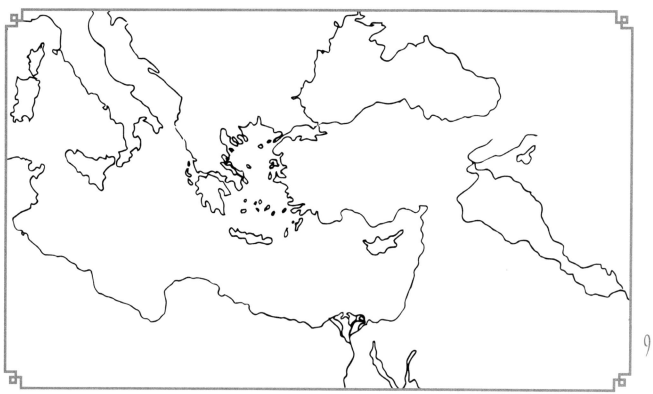

IN THE SPACE PROVIDED BELOW,
LABEL EACH LOCATION ON THE MAP AND RECORD FACTS FROM THE TEXT.

Croton	
Egypt	
Miletus	
Samos	
Syria	
Tyre	

LESSON 2

◠ CREATIVITY & CRITICAL THINKING UNLEASHED

PYTHAGORAS

YOU LIVE IN THE FIRST CENTURY AD. At this moment, you gather with fellow members of a secretive society which follows The Pythagorean Way. You were drawn to them because you have an overwhelming desire to belong to a community, and although you do not really understand why you must follow certain instructions and engage in certain practices, you do your best to obey your leaders and respect their authority.

Today, they discuss a new sect of Judaism currently blazing across the landscape. It is called simply: "The Way."

As a member of The Pythagorean Way, you were taught that you live many lives, and after you die you leave your present body and inhabit another (metempsychosis): maybe a human, maybe a giraffe, or perhaps a bush.

But followers of The Way hold that each person lives only one life on earth, and then stands before an Almighty God to give an account for how he or she lived.

You prefer the idea of coming back again and again, especially since there is always the possibility you may return as royalty, or something powerful, like a lion. But you cannot merely reject this sect's claim because of one disturbing fact: their leader was publicly crucified and now many witnesses—hundreds, in fact—report that He has risen from the dead. They have seen Him.

As you listen to your leaders discuss strategies to combat the defection of fellow members who are leaving to follow Jesus, the leader of "The Way," what do you hear?

Your Assignment: Describe the scene and tell what happens.

Background: Is there anything you would like to say to set up the scene? Do you want to tell us more about your background, and why you were drawn to the Pythagoreans?

The Dialogue: What do your leaders say? Does anyone voice any objections? If so, how does the group respond?

Incorporate your senses into your writing:

- ◠ What do you see?
- ◠ What do you hear?
- ◠ What do you smell?
- ◠ What temperature and textures do you encounter?
- ◠ Are you sharing a meal as you listen? If so, how does it taste?

Set the timer for fifteen minutes, use the back of this page, and *write!*

LESSON 2

CREATIVITY & CRITICAL THINKING UNLEASHED

12

PYTHAGORAS

MEET THE PHILOSOPHER
XENOPHANES

Title(s):

Famous Quote:

WHAT MADE XENOPHANES DIFFERENT FROM OTHER INFLUENTIAL THINKERS BEFORE HIM?

HOW DO WE KNOW WHAT HE BELIEVED?

WHAT DID HE IDENTIFY AS THE ARCHE OR ESSENTIAL SUBSTANCE OF LIFE?

NAME THREE NATURAL PHENOMENA ABOUT WHICH XENOPHANES WROTE.

LESSON 3

HIS STORY UNFOLDS

WHAT WERE SOME OPINIONS HE EXPRESSED THAT CHALLENGED THE CULTURE OF HIS DAY?

DO YOU NOTE ANY SIMILARITIES BETWEEN HIS CULTURE AND OURS? IF SO, EXPLAIN.

WHAT IS ONE POSSIBLE REASON ARISTOTLE DISREGARDED XENOPHANES' WORK AS A NATURAL SCIENTIST?

HOW DO HIS BELIEFS COMPARE TO A BIBLICAL WORLDVIEW? IN WHAT WAYS ARE THEY SIMILAR? IN WHAT WAYS ARE THEY DIFFERENT?

EXPLORE HIS WORLD
XENOPHANES

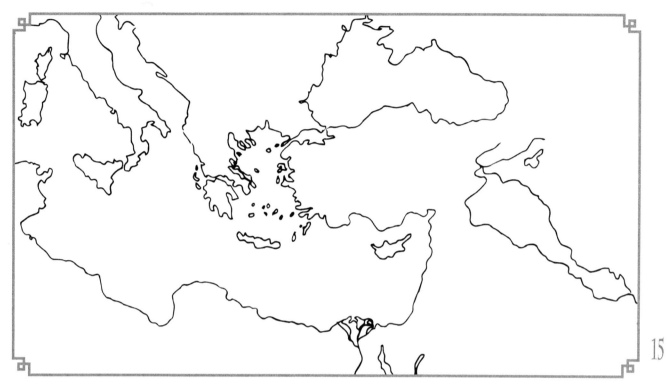

LOCATE & LABEL EACH OF THE FOLLOWING BODIES OF WATER ON YOUR MAP:

| Adriatic Sea | Agean Sea | Black Sea |
| Ionian Sea | Mediterranean Sea | Red Sea |

LOCATE & LABEL EACH DESTINATION LISTED BELOW—EXCLUDING GREECE—
AND RECORD FACTS FROM THE LESSON IN THE SPACE PROVIDED.

Colophon	
Greece	
Sicily	
Elea	

LESSON 3

CREATIVITY & CRITICAL THINKING UNLEASHED

XENOPHANES

WHILE VISITING YOUR BEST FRIEND'S FARM, you walk past the barn on the way to the farmhouse and chance to hear a conversation.

You stealthily approach the barn door and peek inside, undetected. There you watch as a pig boasts to a horse and a cow that he would make a better god than they.

What do you see? What does he say? And how do they reply?

Your Assignment: Describe the scene and tell what happens.

Background: Is there anything you need to say to set up the scene?

The Dialogue:

- Do you stay hidden or do you enter their conversation?
- What does the pig say?
- How does the horse reply?
- Does the cow express her opinion?

Incorporate your senses into your writing:

- What do you see?
- What do you hear?
- What do you smell?
- What temperature and textures do you encounter?
- Do you munch on a farm fresh apple or twirl a stalk of hay between your lips as you listen? Describe how it tastes.

Set the timer for fifteen minutes, use the back of this page, and *write!*

LESSON 3

CREATIVITY & CRITICAL THINKING UNLEASHED

18

XENOPHANES

MEET THE PHILOSOPHER
HERACLITUS

Title(s):

Famous Quote:

WHAT DO WE THINK HERACLITUS MEANT BY THE QUOTE RECORDED ABOVE?

HOW DO WE KNOW WHAT HE BELIEVED?

HOW WERE FRAGMENTS OF HERACLITUS' WRITING DIFFERENT FROM THE FRAGMENTS OF OTHER PRE-SOCRATIC PHILOSOPHERS?

WHAT NEW TECHNICAL TERM DID HERACLITUS INTRODUCE INTO PHILOSOPHICAL DISCUSSION, AND HOW IS IT DIFFERENT FROM THE ARCHE?

LESSON 4

∾ HIS STORY UNFOLDS

WHAT IS ONE COSMOLOGICAL THEORY HERACLITUS PROPOSED REGARDING THE SUN AND MOON?

WHAT DID HERACLITUS SAY ABOUT PYTHAGORAS AND THE POETS HOMER AND HESIOD?

WHAT STORIES ARE TOLD ABOUT HOW HERACLITUS DIED?

HOW DO HIS BELIEFS COMPARE TO A BIBLICAL WORLDVIEW? IN WHAT WAYS ARE THEY SIMILAR? IN WHAT WAYS ARE THEY DIFFERENT?

EXPLORE HIS WORLD
HERACLITUS

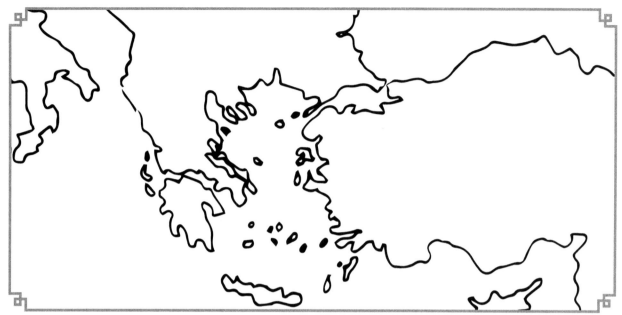

LABEL THE LOCATION OF EACH OF THE SEVEN CHURCHES ADDRESSED IN REVELATION 1:19-3:22. WHAT PRAISE AND/OR WARNINGS WERE GIVEN TO EACH CHURCH? RECORD DETAILS IN THE SPACE BELOW.

Ephesus	
Laodicea	
Pergamon	
Philadelphia	
Sardis	
Smyrna	
Thyatira	

LESSON 4

CREATIVITY & CRITICAL THINKING UNLEASHED

HERACLITUS

As you walk down a road in Ephesus, you pass the home of a noble family. From inside, you hear voices engaged in a heated discussion. At first you can only pick up a word here or there, but soon the volume increases.

Concerned, you cautiously move toward the side of the house and peer in a window. You see two men who are obviously brothers. You gradually discern that they are arguing over who should be king.

What happens next?

Your Assignment: Describe the scene and tell what happens.

Background: What do you need to tell your audience to setup the scene?

The Dialogue: What bits of their conversation do you capture?

Your Senses:

- What do you see?
- What do you hear?
- What do you smell?
- What temperature and textures do you encounter?
- What do you taste?

Set the timer for fifteen minutes, use the back of this page, and *write!*

LESSON 4

CREATIVITY & CRITICAL THINKING UNLEASHED

24

HERACLITUS

MEET THE PHILOSOPHER
PARMENIDES

Title(s):

Famous Quote:

Is the title given to Parmenides appropriate? Why or why not?

What is the title and format of Parmenides philosophical treatise?

How did Parmenides claim to have received the revelation contained in his treatise?

Who were the two prominent Eleatic philosophers who defended and extended Parmenides' doctrines? What did you learn about them?

LESSON 5

◦ HIS STORY UNFOLDS

WHAT ARE THE NAMES OF THE TWO WAYS OF INQUIRY PRESENTED BY THE GODDESS PARMENIDES CLAIMS TO HAVE ENCOUNTERED, AND WHAT SUMMARY STATEMENT DOES SHE MAKE ABOUT EACH?

WHEN WE LOOK AT THE PRE-SOCRATIC AND POST-SOCRATIC PHILOSOPHERS WITH RESPECT TO THEIR EXTANT WRITINGS, WHAT TWO EXTREMES AND RESULTING PROBLEMS DO WE TYPICALLY ENCOUNTER?

PARMENIDES REJECTS THE EMPIRICIST'S BELIEF THAT TRUE KNOWLEDGE IS GAINED THROUGH THE SENSES. WHAT DOES HE EMBRACE INSTEAD?

WHAT WAS PARMENIDES' CENTRAL THESIS AND THE FOUR CONCISE CONCLUSIONS PRESENTED IN HIS TREATISE ACCORDING TO PROFESSOR COHEN?

PARMENIDES

◈ EXPLORE HIS WORLD
PARMENIDES

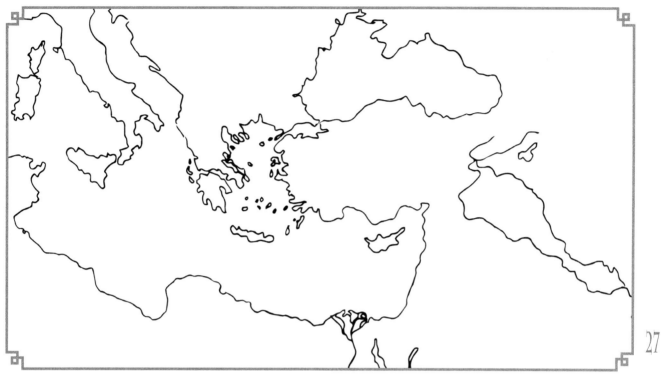

LABEL EACH OF THE FOLLOWING LOCATIONS ON YOUR MAP:

Tyrrhenian Sea　　　　Athens　　　　Elea

IN THE SPACE PROVIDED BELOW, RECORD RELEVANT FACTS FROM THE TEXT.

Greek Colonies	
Elea	
Athens	

LESSON 5

CREATIVITY & CRITICAL THINKING UNLEASHED

PARMENIDES

YOU MEET AN ANGEL who tells you there is a way that seems right, but in the end it leads to death. He sweeps you off your feet and carries you away to a clearing surrounded by a sunlit forest. Then he sets your feet on a narrow winding trail that disappears into the trees.

"This is the path of life," he tells you. "Do not stray from it."

Then he disappears.

What happens next? Do you stay on the path? Tell us about your experience.

Your Assignment: Describe the scene and tell what happens.

Background: Is there anything you need to tell us to set up the scene?

Incorporate your senses into your writing:

- What do you see?
- What do you hear?
- What do you smell?
- What temperatures and textures do you encounter?
- What do you taste?

Set the timer for fifteen minutes, use the back of this page, and *write!*

LESSON 5

CREATIVITY & CRITICAL THINKING UNLEASHED

30

PARMENIDES

～ MEET THE PHILOSOPHER
EMPEDOCLES

Title(s):

Famous Quote:

WHAT FOUR ELEMENTS AND TWO FORCES DID EMPEDOCLES IDENTIFY IN HIS COSMOGONY?

WHAT EXCITING DISCOVERY RELATED TO EMPEDOCLES WAS MADE IN THE 1990S IN THE STRASBOURG UNIVERSITY LIBRARY? WHAT SIGNIFICANT CONTROVERSY DID IT INFLAME?

WHAT CULT DID EMPEDOCLES SUPPOSEDLY BETRAY THROUGH HIS POETRY, AND WHAT DID THE CULT MEMBERS DO AFTER HIS DEPARTURE?

WHAT "TERRIBLE TRANSGRESSION" DID EMPEDOCLES SAY HE COMMITTED THAT CONDEMNED HIM TO BE "BORN THROUGHOUT TIME IN ALL MANNERS OF MORTAL FORMS"? WHAT UNBIBLICAL BELIEF WAS USED AS THE BASIS FOR JUDGING THE ACT TO BE TERRIBLE?

LESSON 6

◆ HIS STORY UNFOLDS

Empedocles refused a crown and instituted democracy in Sicily. What is the difference between an oligarchy, a democracy, and a republic?

What stories did you learn about how Empedocles may have died?

What is significant about Empedocles' bronze sandal?

Empedocles was one of three major pre-Socratic philosophers among the Pluralists. What is the difference between a monist and a pluralist?

EMPEDOCLES

◦ EXPLORE HIS WORLD
EMPEDOCLES

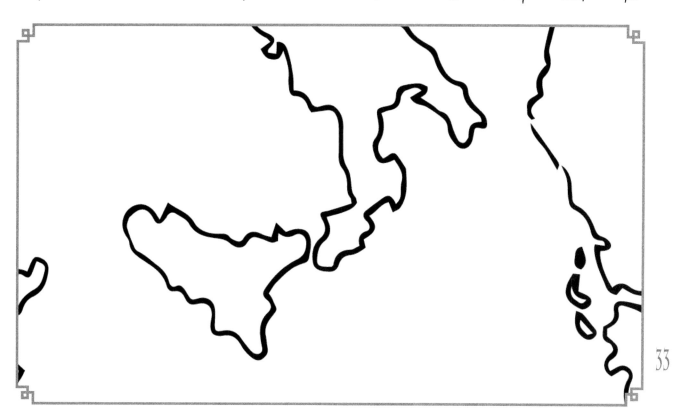

ON THE MAP ABOVE, LABEL THE LOCATION OF THE FOLLOWING VOLCANOES:

| Mount Etna | Mount Stromboli | Mount Vesuvius |

IN THE SPACE PROVIDED BELOW, RECORD AT LEAST THREE THINGS YOU LEARNED ABOUT MOUNT ETNA.

LESSON 6

CREATIVITY & CRITICAL THINKING UNLEASHED

EMPEDOCLES

"Doctor, Democrat, & The First Evolutionist"

THE PHILOSOPHER EMPEDOCLES IMAGINED a horrific scene as the moment that brought us into existence, driven by the impersonal forces of Love and Strife. According to his account, a vortex created by Strife separated the roots of earth, wind, fire, and water into random mixtures that produced a variety of monstrosities—including man-faced oxen and oxen-faced men. Many of these beasts became extinct; those that proved viable remained and eventually reproduced.

The creation account given in the book of Genesis records a scene that could not be more different. Random selection is replaced with inconceivably brilliant design. Grotesque chance combinations are replaced by gloriously crafted creation—with the crown jewel fearfully and wonderfully made.

Imagine for a moment that you are one of the heavenly host privileged to be present to witness God speak this world into its uncorrupted, perfect existence. Review Genesis 1:

> 1 In the beginning, God created the heavens and the earth. 2 The earth was without form and void, and darkness was over the face of the deep. And the Spirit of God was hovering over the face of the waters.
>
> 3 And God said, "Let there be light," and there was light. 4 And God saw that the light was good. And God separated the light from the darkness. 5 God called the light Day, and the darkness he called Night. And there was evening and there was morning, the first day.
>
> 6 And God said, "Let there be an expanse[a] in the midst of the waters, and let it separate the waters from the waters." 7 And God made[b] the expanse and separated the waters that were under the expanse from the waters that were above the expanse. And it was so. 8 And God called the expanse Heaven.[c] And there was evening and there was morning, the second day.
>
> 9 And God said, "Let the waters under the heavens be gathered together into one place, and let the dry land appear." And it was so. 10 God called the dry land Earth,[d] and the waters that were gathered together he called Seas. And God saw that it was good.
>
> 11 And God said, "Let the earth sprout vegetation, plants[e] yielding seed, and fruit trees bearing fruit in which is their seed, each according to its kind, on the earth." And it was so. 12 The earth brought forth vegetation, plants yielding seed according to their own kinds, and trees bearing fruit in which is their seed, each according to its kind. And God saw that it was good. 13 And there was evening and there was morning, the third day.
>
> 14 And God said, "Let there be lights in the expanse of the heavens to separate the day from the night. And let them be for signs and for seasons,[f] and for days and years, 15 and let them be lights in the expanse of the heavens to give light upon the earth." And it was so. 16 And God made the two great lights—the greater light to rule the day and the lesser light to rule the night—and the stars. 17 And God set them in the expanse of the heavens to give light on the earth, 18 to rule over the day and over the night, and to separate the light from the darkness. And God saw that it was good. 19 And there was evening and there was morning, the fourth day.
>
> 20 And God said, "Let the waters swarm with swarms of living creatures, and let birds[g] fly above the earth across the expanse of the heavens." 21 So God created the great sea creatures and every living creature that moves, with which the waters swarm, according to their kinds, and every winged bird according to its kind. And God saw that

LESSON 6

it was good. 22 And God blessed them, saying, "Be fruitful and multiply and fill the waters in the seas, and let birds multiply on the earth." 23 And there was evening and there was morning, the fifth day.

24 And God said, "Let the earth bring forth living creatures according to their kinds—livestock and creeping things and beasts of the earth according to their kinds." And it was so. 25 And God made the beasts of the earth according to their kinds and the livestock according to their kinds, and everything that creeps on the ground according to its kind. And God saw that it was good.

26 Then God said, "Let us make man[h] in our image, after our likeness. And let them have dominion over the fish of the sea and over the birds of the heavens and over the livestock and over all the earth and over every creeping thing that creeps on the earth."

27 So God created man in his own image,
   in the image of God he created him;
   male and female he created them.

28 And God blessed them. And God said to them, "Be fruitful and multiply and fill the earth and subdue it, and have dominion over the fish of the sea and over the birds of the heavens and over every living thing that moves on the earth." 29 And God said, "Behold, I have given you every plant yielding seed that is on the face of all the earth, and every tree with seed in its fruit. You shall have them for food. 30 And to every beast of the earth and to every bird of the heavens and to everything that creeps on the earth, everything that has the breath of life, I have given every green plant for food." And it was so. 31 And God saw everything that he had made, and behold, it was very good. And there was evening and there was morning, the sixth day.

Your Assignment: Imagine yourself in the scene and describe it.

- When God speaks, does light explode?
- What hush falls about the heavenly host when God places His imprint on His creation in the unique form of man—who receives the privilege of bearing the very image of God?
- What is stunningly beautiful or ridiculously funny?

Incorporate all five senses into your writing:

- What do you see?
- What do you hear?
- What do you smell?
- What temperature and textures do you encounter?
- What do you taste?

Grab a sheet of paper, set the timer for fifteen minutes, and ***write!***

EMPEDOCLES

MEET THE PHILOSOPHER
PROTAGORAS

Title(s):

Famous Quote:

WHO WERE THE FIRST SOPHISTS, AND IN WHAT WAY WAS PROTAGORAS DIFFERENT FROM THEM?

WHAT IS ONE BOAST PROTAGORAS MADE ABOUT HIS PERSUASIVE SPEAKING SKILL?

HOW MUCH DID PROTAGORAS CHARGE HIS STUDENTS, AND WHY WERE WEALTHY ATHENIANS WILLING TO PAY SUCH HIGH FEES TO SOPHISTS?

WHAT STORY IS TOLD ABOUT THE RELATIONSHIP BETWEEN PROTAGORAS AND THE PHILOSOPHER DEMOCRITUS? DO YOU THINK IT IS TRUE? WHY OR WHY NOT?

LESSON 7

❦ HIS STORY UNFOLDS

WHAT APOLOGIA DID THE SOPHIST GORGIAS PRESENT ON BEHALF OF HELEN OF TROY?

WHAT TWO EVENTS ARE DESCRIBED THAT INVOLVED BOTH PROTAGORAS AND PERICLES?

PERICLES HAD A REPUTATION FOR POSSESSING POWERFUL PERSUASIVE SPEAKING SKILLS. WHAT WAS SAID ABOUT HIS ABILITY TO INFLUENCE HIS AUDIENCE? CITE ONE EXAMPLE OF HOW HE USED HIS SKILLS TO MANIPULATE PUBLIC OPINION.

WHAT STATEMENT DID PROTAGORAS MAKE ABOUT THE EXISTENCE OF GOD?

PROTAGORAS

◈ EXPLORE HIS WORLD
PROTAGORAS

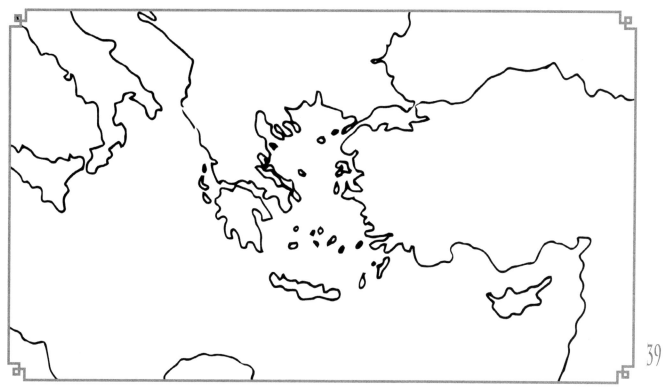

On the map above, label the contemporary boundaries of Thrace by identifying the approximate location of each item listed below:

| Sea of Marmara | Agean Sea | Black Sea |
| Rhodope Mountains | Balkan Mountains |

In the space provided below, (1) label each location on the map and (2) record facts from the text.

Abdera	
Athens	
Sicily	

LESSON 7

◐ CREATIVITY & CRITICAL THINKING UNLEASHED

PROTAGORAS
"The Sophist"

IMAGINE YOU WERE HIRED BY A PRESTIGIOUS LAW FIRM. You are the lead attorney in a high-profile trial. The senior partner called you into his office this morning and said that if you win this trial, he will make you a partner in the firm.

The defendant comes from an extremely affluent family. He has been charged with savagely murdering his father. Although several family members and friends testified against him, as you worked closely with him to prepare for this trial, he convinced you that he is innocent.

Ever since you were a child, you dreamed of being a hero and defending "the underdog." You poured your best into this trial. All that remains for you to do now is your closing statement.

Before you approach the jury, you turn toward the defendant. His pupils appear strangely dilated, his eyes black, and his expression unsettling. He leans toward you. Only you hear as he whispers a hideous confession. Then he slaps you on the back and grins.

What happens next?

Your Assignment: Imagine yourself in the scene and describe it.

- ◐ What did he say?
- ◐ What are your thoughts?
- ◐ What will you say to the jury?

Incorporate all five senses into your writing:

- ◐ What do you see?
- ◐ What do you hear?
- ◐ What do you smell?
- ◐ What do you taste?
- ◐ What temperature and textures do you encounter?

Set the timer for fifteen minutes, use the back of this page, and *write!*

LESSON 7

CREATIVITY & CRITICAL THINKING UNLEASHED

42

PROTAGORAS

MEET THE PHILOSOPHER
DEMOCRITUS

Title(s):

Famous Quote:

WHERE WAS DEMOCRITUS BORN, WHAT WAS HIS FAMILY BACKGROUND, AND WHO DID DIOGENES LAERTIUS SAY WERE HIS FIRST MENTORS?

WHAT ARE THREE PLACES TO WHICH DEMOCRITUS WAS SAID TO HAVE TRAVELED?

HOW DID DEMOCRITUS SPEND HIS INHERITANCE, AND, ONCE IT WAS GONE, WHAT DID HE DO TO EARN AN INCOME?

WHAT AMAZING THEORY IS DEMOCRITUS KNOWN FOR POPULARIZING AND INTRODUCING INTO THE GREAT CONVERSATION?

LESSON 8

～ HIS STORY UNFOLDS

BRIEFLY EXPLAIN ZENO'S DICHOTOMY PARADOX AND NAME THE FORM OF NON-BEING THAT DEMOCRITUS USED TO REFUTE IT.

WHO ARE SOME OF THE BRILLIANT THINKERS FROM HISTORY WHO BELIEVED ATOMIC THEORY ORIGINATED WITH MOCHUS THE PHOENICIAN, A/K/A MOSES THE LAWGIVER?

WHAT DID DEMOCRITUS SAY ABOUT THE CREATION OF THE UNIVERSE AND THE CONSISTENCY OF THE HUMAN SOUL?

WHAT WILD TALE IS TOLD ABOUT DEMOCRITUS' DEMISE?

DEMOCRITUS

◦⁓ EXPLORE HIS WORLD
DEMOCRITUS

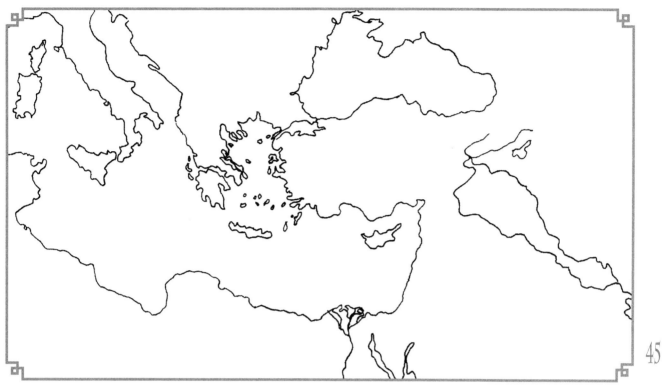

ON THE MAP ABOVE, LABEL EACH OF THE FOLLOWING LOCATIONS:

| Abdera | Athens | Miletus |
| Egypt | | Persia |

IN THE TABLE BELOW, RECORD WHAT YOU HAVE LEARNED ABOUT EACH LOCATION.

ABDERA	
ATHENS	
MILETUS	
EGYPT	
PERSIA	

LESSON 8

◌ CREATIVITY & CRITICAL THINKING UNLEASHED
DEMOCRITUS
"The First Atomist"

YOU WERE ROCK CLIMBING and stumbled upon a narrow opening. It appears to lead to a cave. Curiosity gets the best of you....

You manage to squeeze inside a tunnel faintly illuminated by a stream of sunlight. You crawl along until suddenly you feel yourself falling. Everything is dark.

When you hit the ground, it is surprisingly soft. Light floods your eyes. Blinking, you discover that you have landed in a meadow of wildflowers.

How did you get here? What clues you in to the fact that you have entered a parallel world?

What happens next?

Your Assignment: Imagine yourself in the scene and describe it.

Background: Is there anything you need to tell us to set up the scene?

Incorporate all five senses into your writing:

- ◌ What do you see?
- ◌ What do you hear?
- ◌ What do you smell?
- ◌ What do you taste?
- ◌ What temperature and textures do you encounter?

You have 15 minutes. *Write!*

LESSON 8

DEMOCRITUS

WRITE ✦ THINK ✦ SPEAK
JOURNAL

WRITE SKILLFULLY

JOURNAL

For your first assignment, ponder and write your answers to three of the most profound questions philosophy seeks to address. Set a timer for 30 minutes and write the best answers you can in the time allotted.

1. Where did I come from and why am I here?

LESSON 1

~ Write Skillfully
# JOURNAL

2. Why is there evil, suffering, and death?

3. Is there hope for my future? If not, why? If so, what is the source of that hope?

THINK CRITICALLY

JOURNAL

1. How do you define learning? (See p. 5)

2. What have you studied extensively—an academic subject, music, technology, or something you enjoy in your free time—and how did you learn about it? (Write about the process.)

3. What can inspire you to develop your memory "muscle"?

LESSON 1

~Speak Articulately
JOURNAL

1. What does it mean to have a transcendent goal?

2. Can you identify a prize for which you would be willing to suffer?

3. What are some things you can do that will help you persevere as you pursue that prize?

WRITE SKILLFULLY

JOURNAL

Imagine your audience asking the following questions as they listen to you speak. How will you answer them? Let your answers guide your writing.

1. Why should I listen to your speech?

LESSON 2

~ WRITE SKILLFULLY
# JOURNAL

2. When and where did this person live?

   Provide setting details to help your reader understand the times in which your subject lived.

3. Who is this person?

   Who were his/her parents? Where was he/she educated? Did he/she marry? Did he/she have children?

PYTHAGORAS

WRITE SKILLFULLY
JOURNAL

4. What is significant about this person?

   What impact did your subject have upon the world? What contributions did he/she make? Inventions? Ideas? Influence?

5. How did this person live?

   Provide details regarding his/her lifestyle choices and the benefits or consequences that resulted. How did his/her story end?

LESSON 2

~Think Critically
JOURNAL

As you consider the reliability of any source, begin by asking a few key questions. Write answers to the following questions for the text of your choice.

1. What do you know about this author?

2. Who is the author's intended audience and how might that audience influence the content?

3. What are the main points discussed and/or arguments presented?

PYTHAGORAS

THINK CRITICALLY
JOURNAL

4. What assumptions does the author make about his or her audience and the information presented?

5. What evidence, if any, does the author supply to support his or her arguments and conclusions?

LESSON 2

Think Critically
JOURNAL

6. Do you perceive any weaknesses in the arguments presented? If so, describe them.

WRITE SKILLFULLY

JOURNAL

These questions will help you prepare to write the "terrible" first draft of your speech.

1. Why are you passionate about your subject?

2. Who is your target audience? Describe the typical ages, interests, and educational background of your audience.

LESSON 3

✑ Write Skillfully
JOURNAL

3. How can you make this subject interesting and significant to your audience?

4. What background information is necessary for your audience to understand your subject?

XENOPHANES

WRITE SKILLFULLY
JOURNAL

5. What stories, evidence, or examples can you use to support any conclusion you make about your subject?

6. What are some questions your audience is likely to ask? How can you answer them?

WRITE SKILLFULLY
JOURNAL

7. Write three possible openers you can use to capture the attention of your audience. (Consider using an analogy, relevant quote, Scripture, engaging story, or shocking fact.)

8. What do you think is the best way to organize the information presented in your speech? Why?

XENOPHANES

WRITE SKILLFULLY
JOURNAL

9. What are some possible "bows" for your speech?

LESSON 3

～Think Critically
JOURNAL

Now it is your turn to engage in epistemology—and answer these questions:

1. What are three things beyond your ability to know for certain?

2. What are three things that you only know because the Bible revealed them to you?

3. Can you think of a time when your senses deceived you? Describe it.

XENOPHANES

WRITE SKILLFULLY

JOURNAL

Heraclitus played with words. He used a variety of stylistic techniques to enhance his writing, lacing it with multiple meanings, making it pleasing to his reader's eye and lyrical to his listener's ear.

Now it is your turn to play with words. Experiment with three techniques that can refine and enhance your writing: PAUSE, PLAY, PRUNE.

1. In the midst of media madness, the skillful writer employs the pause. Lets things breathe. Creates space. Take a paragraph from your "terrible" first draft (or another excerpt of your original writing), and try to edit your sentence lengths to add excitement. Employ the "Last-First-Middle" rule.

LESSON 4

～ Write Skillfully
JOURNAL

2. Now PLAY with that paragraph! Add a touch of alliteration.

3. Can you weave in a simile or metaphor? Experiment. Be free! (Remember: this is only your "terrible" first draft. You will polish it later.)

HERACLITUS

THINK CRITICALLY
JOURNAL

1. There is a difference between having a opinion that is different than another person's opinion, and arguing that truth is different for you than it is for someone else. Write at least a paragraph giving your opinion on something about which you feel strongly—but is still your personal opinion and does not rise to the level of absolute truth.

    (For example, "I really believe and experience has taught me that writing is one of the best ways you can discover what you think about a subject....")

LESSON 4

Think Critically
JOURNAL

2. Can you think of a time someone has told you, *"That may be true for you, but it is not true for me"*? If so, briefly describe your experience.

3. Now that you have studied the Law of Non-Contradiction, how might you respond to someone who made the statement in question two? (Remember to answer with gentleness and respect.)

HERACLITUS

WRITE SKILLFULLY

JOURNAL

First impressions are powerful. Whether accurate or not, they form our opinions of people, places, and things, and once that impression has been made, it is difficult to shake.

1. Write about a time when someone made a first impression that later proved to be false.

   (For example, you met someone who you thought was arrogant but later discovered was only very shy.)

LESSON 5

Write Skillfully
JOURNAL

2. Write about a time when you made a poor first impression on someone. Were you able to overcome that first impression? If so, how?

3. It is time to play again. Write a paragraph and overuse exclamation marks!!!! Then read your paragraph aloud to someone the way it is written. Be dramatic!

PARMENIDES

THINK CRITICALLY
JOURNAL

Now that you have been introduced to ontology basics, answer these questions:

1. What is one core belief related to existence to which you are committed?

   (For example: "God exists.")

2. How do you think that belief might influence your investigation as you ask, "What exists?"

LESSON 5

Think Critically
JOURNAL

3. What standard will you use to determine the validity of any answers you encounter, and why is that important?

4. Describe something that you cannot perceive with your senses but which you firmly believe exists. Why do you believe it exists?

PARMENIDES

WRITE SKILLFULLY

JOURNAL

Developing writers need a safe place to share work and receive honest feedback and encouragement.

1. Can you think of a time when you took a risk and tried something new...and it didn't go well. Write about it.

LESSON 6

~ WRITE SKILLFULLY
# JOURNAL

2. What do you most want from a person when he or she gives you feedback on your writing?

3. What do you absolutely *not* want a person to do when giving you feedback on your writing? Why?

4. Who is your favorite person to share your writing with? Why?

Think Critically
JOURNAL

In lesson five, we explored ontology and examined three foundational questions of existence. Now answer these ontological questions as they relate to chance:

1. Does chance exist? (Does it have being?) Why or why not?

2. If it exists, of what material is it made? (Yes. This is a trick question, intended to make you think!)

3. How does it relate to other things that exist? (Does it have the power to influence the things around it?)

LESSON 6

~ Speak Articulately
JOURNAL

After you have enjoyed watching a few interpretive speeches, answer the following questions:

1. Of the speeches you watched, what was your favorite and why?

2. If you had to perform one of the speeches you watched, which one would you select and why?

3. Of the speeches you watched, which one do you think had the greatest impact and why?

WRITE SKILLFULLY

JOURNAL

Truth runs like a thread through the patchwork of readers' comments. Give special attention to comments repeated by multiple readers.

1. If you had multiple readers, did they repeat the same suggestion or observation? If so, what did they say? If not, were any suggestions contradictory? Record them below.

2. What was the most difficult feedback to read? What made it so?

3. What were the most valuable comments you received on your peer critique, and what made them valuable?

LESSON 7

Think Critically
JOURNAL

In Lesson Seven, we explored the two primary types of fallacies: formal and informal. Here is an opportunity to experiment with informal fallacies.

1. Create a story in which a red herring is used to distract someone from something significant.

PROTAGORAS

THINK CRITICALLY
JOURNAL

2. Create a playful example of equivocation.

3. In Lesson Seven, you were introduced to a formal fallacy known as a syllogism. Does the syllogism shared below present a valid line of reasoning? Why or why not?
   (Refer to the explanation given on page 65 to help you answer this question.)

   Some early Greek philosophers were poets.
   Xenophanes was a philosopher.
   Therefore, Xenophanes was a poet.

LESSON 7

～Speak Articulately
JOURNAL

To introduce you to the limited prep category of apologetic speeches, you are asked to take 30 minutes to outline a six-minute speech on the love of God, using only a Bible and blank index cards.

To gain experience with an impromptu speech, select one of the following prompts and, in the space provided below, take 10 minutes to outline a speech. Try presenting in front of a mirror.

    courage   wisdom   honor   foolishness   fear

PROTAGORAS

WRITE SKILLFULLY
JOURNAL

For each pre-Socratic philosopher featured in our lessons, set a timer for 30–45 minutes and freewrite responses to the statements below:

THALES

1. The "big idea(s)" proposed or defended by this philosopher were...

2. I was startled to learn....

3. I found myself challenged by the idea that....

LESSON 8

~ Write Skillfully
JOURNAL

4. I strongly disagreed with this philosopher regarding....

5. This philosopher made an impact upon me because....

6. Overall, when I consider the life lived and the ideas presented by this philosopher, my response is...

DEMOCRITUS

WRITE SKILLFULLY
JOURNAL

PYTHAGORAS

1. The "big idea(s)" proposed or defended by this philosopher were...

2. I was startled to learn....

3. I found myself challenged by the idea that....

LESSON 8

~ Write Skillfully
JOURNAL

4. I strongly disagreed with this philosopher regarding....

5. This philosopher made an impact upon me because....

6. Overall, when I consider the life lived and the ideas presented by this philosopher, my response is...

DEMOCRITUS

JOURNAL
Write Skillfully

XENOPHANES

1. The "big idea(s)" proposed or defended by this philosopher were...

2. I was startled to learn....

3. I found myself challenged by the idea that....

LESSON 8

Write Skillfully
JOURNAL

4. I strongly disagreed with this philosopher regarding....

5. This philosopher made an impact upon me because....

6. Overall, when I consider the life lived and the ideas presented by this philosopher, my response is...

DEMOCRITUS

WRITE SKILLFULLY
JOURNAL

HERACLITUS

1. The "big idea(s)" proposed or defended by this philosopher were...

2. I was startled to learn....

3. I found myself challenged by the idea that....

LESSON 8

~ WRITE SKILLFULLY
JOURNAL

4. I strongly disagreed with this philosopher regarding....

5. This philosopher made an impact upon me because....

6. Overall, when I consider the life lived and the ideas presented by this philosopher, my response is...

DEMOCRITUS

WRITE SKILLFULLY
JOURNAL

PARMENIDES

1. The "big idea(s)" proposed or defended by this philosopher were...

2. I was startled to learn....

3. I found myself challenged by the idea that....

LESSON 8

Write Skillfully
JOURNAL

4. I strongly disagreed with this philosopher regarding....

5. This philosopher made an impact upon me because....

6. Overall, when I consider the life lived and the ideas presented by this philosopher, my response is...

DEMOCRITUS

Write Skillfully
JOURNAL

EMPEDOCLES

1. The "big idea(s)" proposed or defended by this philosopher were...

2. I was startled to learn....

3. I found myself challenged by the idea that....

LESSON 8

~ Write Skillfully
JOURNAL

4. I strongly disagreed with this philosopher regarding....

5. This philosopher made an impact upon me because....

6. Overall, when I consider the life lived and the ideas presented by this philosopher, my response is...

DEMOCRITUS

WRITE SKILLFULLY
JOURNAL

PROTAGORAS

1. The "big idea(s)" proposed or defended by this philosopher were...

2. I was startled to learn....

3. I found myself challenged by the idea that....

LESSON 8

～ WRITE SKILLFULLY
JOURNAL

4. I strongly disagreed with this philosopher regarding....

5. This philosopher made an impact upon me because....

6. Overall, when I consider the life lived and the ideas presented by this philosopher, my response is...

DEMOCRITUS

WRITE SKILLFULLY
JOURNAL

DEMOCRITUS

1. The "big idea(s)" proposed or defended by this philosopher were...

2. I was startled to learn....

3. I found myself challenged by the idea that....

LESSON 8

~ Write Skillfully
JOURNAL

4. I strongly disagreed with this philosopher regarding....

5. This philosopher made an impact upon me because....

6. Overall, when I consider the life lived and the ideas presented by this philosopher, my response is...

DEMOCRITUS

WRITE SKILLFULLY
JOURNAL

For your final WRITE assignment, revisit the big three philosophical questions. Has your perspective changed? Does a biblical worldview now seem more credible or less?:

1. Where did I come from and why am I here?

LESSON 8

～Write Skillfully
JOURNAL

2. Why is there evil, suffering, and death?

3. Is there hope for my future? If not, why? If so, what is the source of that hope?

Think Critically
JOURNAL

In light of what we have learned in our lessons, consider the presuppositions listed below and write a response.

1. Extreme faith in God is dangerous to your health. (See lesson two.)

2. Chance played a key role in the creation of the universe.

LESSON 8

Think Critically
JOURNAL

3. The ancient Greek philosophers were strictly materialists.

DEMOCRITUS

SPEAK ARTICULATELY
JOURNAL

You completed a tour of competitive speech categories and forms, and you have pondered the power and purposes for the spoken word.

1. What is your favorite speech category? Why?

2. In what category do you feel best equipped to perform?

3. What do you see as the right motivation for developing speaking skills?

LESSON 8

∽ Speak Articulately
JOURNAL

4. Let's get personal now. How do you plan to honor God with the gift of spoken communication that He has given you?

CHECKLISTS

PRE-WRITING CHECKLIST NO. 1

S T A R T

Begin the Discovery Process

PRE-WRITING

When you first get started, your writing experience may defy the regulations you attempt to place upon it. You envision one smooth stream of thought; your words plunge you into an unexpected downpour.

There is a fine balance to maintain during the creative process. You need to start the flow and keep it flowing—and yet prevent it from overflowing and drowning you. And, at some point, you have to shut off the spigot, peer into the barrel, and evaluate what you have collected.

Think "ebb and flow." Be open to creative ideas—even as you are wise, knowing those ideas must be shaped into clear, precise, comprehendible communication.

☐	1. Did you brainstorm ideas? (Clustering, freewriting, mapping?)
☐	2. Is the subject you have selected significant?
☐	3. Are you passionate about it?
☐	4. Did you identify your target audience?
☐	5. Can you make this subject interesting and significant to them?
☐	6. Is there enough information available on this subject to write a compelling piece?
☐	7. Did you begin a list of questions for further research?

WRITER'S CHECKLIST NO. 2
SUBSTANCE

What is your message? Why should we listen?

WHEN YOU COLLECT CONTENT, YOUR PRIMARY CONCERN IS SIGNIFICANCE— harvest information worthy of the time you will invest crafting and presenting your speech, and the time your audience will invest listening to you speak.

Always keep your audience in mind.

1.	Did you make and document significant discoveries about your subject?
2.	Did you consider and collect the background information your audience will need to understand your subject or thesis?
3.	Did you identify at least three credible sources to support your observations or thesis?
4.	Are general concepts or conclusions supported by specific stories, evidence, or examples?
5.	Did you use appropriate qualifiers where necessary?
6.	Did you anticipate and answer your audience's questions and/or objections?
7.	Do all of your sentences tell the truth? (Be careful not to manipulate evidence or information.)

WRITER'S CHECKLIST NO. 3
STRUCTURE

Build a logical framework for your content.

REVIEW "THE ANATOMY OF" FOR THE PAPER THAT YOU ARE PREPARING.
Based upon those instructions, build a structure that will support the substance of your speech.

Do you have all the required components?

	1.	Did you immediately capture your audience's attention with an analogy, relevant Scripture, engaging story, or shocking fact? (Take care to connect your opener to your message.)
	2.	Did you clearly introduce your subject and give your audience a general sense of what to expect from your speech? (In some speech categories, you present a "roadmap" of your speech.)
	3.	Did you chronologically or logically organize information?
	4.	Does each paragraph develop one easily identifiable idea?
	5.	Do you have graceful transitions between ideas, main points, or events?
	6.	Does your conclusion summarize your subject matter or restate your thesis?
	7.	Did you satisfy your audience's expectations and leave them with a sense of completion, urgency, or wonder?

STRUCTURE

WRITER'S CHECKLIST NO. 4
STYLE

Play with your words (but don't lose your message).

AS YOU BEGIN TO ENHANCE YOUR WRITING, REMEMBER THIS RULE:

Last-First-Middle:
Your readers are most likely to remember the last sentence you write,
followed by the first sentence you write,
and, unfortunately,
they frequently forget whatever words you place in the middle.
If you want your audience to remember something,
place it at the end of your paragraph or piece.
Save your best for last!

	1.	Did you create an engaging persona and write with warmth and passion?
	2.	Did you organize your sentences for maximum impact, following the rule of last-first-middle?
	3.	Whenever possible, did you use strong verbs and an active voice?
	4.	There is power in the pause, whether written or spoken. Did you incorporate pauses and rest stops in your writing?
	5.	Did you use a variety of sentence and paragraph lengths, writing for the eye as well as the ear?
	6.	Did you unleash your creativity and play? (Alliteration, analogy, metaphor, and more?)
	7.	Did you boldly and wisely remove all deadwood and unintentional redundancy?

PEER PRE-CRITIQUE CHECKLIST NO. 5
POLISH
Make it shine!

> "And let us not grow weary of doing good, for in due season we will reap, if we do not give up."
>
> Galatians 6:9 ESV

FIRST IMPRESSIONS ARE POWERFUL

Now that you have dressed your draft with style, it is time to polish it for a private presentation.

Whether accurate or not, first impressions form our opinions of people, places, and things. Once an impression has been made, it is difficult to shake.

Just as a person who wishes to be hired would be wise to shower and dress in clean, neat clothing before attending a job interview, the writer who wishes to communicate effectively would be wise to properly format his or her paper before presenting it to an audience.

Carefully review your paper against the items on this polish checklist. By correctly handling these basics, you increase the professionalism of your piece and enhance the overall impression you make upon your reader.

	1. Did you properly **format** your paper? (12 pt Times New Roman, double-spaced, first line of each paragraph indented .5", first page header lists your name, assignment, draft number, word count, and date?)
	2. Did you confirm that each sentence is a **complete** thought? (No sentence fragments are allowed without your instructor's prior approval.)
	3. Did you **capitalize** the start of each sentence, all proper nouns, and all references to God and the Bible, including Scripture, but not including adjectives such as *godly* or *biblical*?
	4. Did you check your **spelling**? (You cannot rely on spell-checkers to catch every word. Proofread carefully, and ask for help from someone in your family.)
	5. Did you close your **quotes**? (If you use quotes within quotes, alternate between double "" and single quotes '' so your reader can follow without getting lost.)
	6. Did you use **parentheses** sparingly and intentionally. (When you use parentheses, it is like whispering to your reader.)
	7. Did you **read your paper aloud** and revise accordingly? Subtle errors and awkward passages difficult to detect when read silently often become obvious when heard.

POLISH

WRITER'S CHECKLIST NO. 6

PEER CRITIQUE
For Your Biographical Narrative

Use these Proof Readers' Symbols as you critique the printed draft (Note: Proof Readers may use alternate symbols for some corrections.)	
⟲	delete
⊙	period
∧	insert text
⥃	insert comma
⊙ (with ∧)	insert colon
⨽	insert semi-colon
※	insert space
⌐⌐	transpose words
≡	capitalize
(lc)	make lowercase
~~	bold
—	italicize
¶	insert paragraph break
❦ ❦ / ❦ ❦	insert single or double quotes
?	insert question mark
◡	close space
(stet)	disregard edit (keep as is)
⊦	move text left
⊣	move text right

FOR THE WRITER

SHARE IN THE SAFETY OF YOUR WRITERS' COMMUNITY

What specific feedback are you looking for from your reader?:
(Ask questions / share thoughts here)

START with encouragement. Name three things you liked about this piece:
1.
2.
3.

FOR THE READER

STRUCTURE ∿ SUBSTANCE ∿ STYLE

Did this piece capture your attention?

What is the central idea (thesis) of the speech?

What are the most significant moments in the life of the subject?
1.
2.
3.

Do you agree that the featured person made a significant contribution to the world?

Did you gain a sense of the time and place in which the person lived (or lives)?

Do you feel you have gained a general understanding of the person featured?

Did you learn about specific choices the person made and the results of those choices?

Are transitions between points logical and graceful?

Did the conclusion summarize and support the central idea (thesis)?

In one word, how did you feel when you finished reading this piece?

PEERCRITIQUE

WRITER'S CHECKLIST NO. 6

PEER CRITIQUE
For Your Biographical Narrative

FOR THE READER

COMPLETE THESE STATEMENTS REGARDING THE WORK'S STRENGTHS:

I found this really interesting...

You changed my mind about...

You really entertained me with...

You engaged my emotions with...

You surprised me by...

COMPLETE THESE STATEMENTS REGARDING ANY WEAKNESSES:

I found my attention drifting when...

I felt insulted by...

I found it confusing when...

You did not persuade me of your central idea (thesis) because...

I still wanted to know more about...

NEXT STEPS

How can the writer improve this piece?

LESSON 10

GRADING CRITERIA CHECKLIST NO. 7

EVALUATION
The Final Feedback

> "And let us not grow weary of doing good,
> for in due season we will reap,
> if we do not give up."
>
> Galatians 6:9 ESV

	SUBSTANCE	Poor 1	Fair 2	Good 3	Very Good 4	Excellent 5
1.	Significant and thought-provoking subject matter					
2.	Carefully worded; avoids clichés or undefined jargon					
3.	Well-researched with several credible and properly cited sources					
4.	General concepts supported by specific evidence/stories/examples					
5.	Does not overstate claims; appropriate qualifiers used wherever necessary					
6.	Writer anticipates and addresses potential reader's objections					
7.	All sentences tell the truth.					
	STRUCTURE	Poor 1	Fair 2	Good 3	Very Good 4	Excellent 5
8.	Properly formatted (12 pt Times New Roman, double-spaced, first line .5" indented)					
9.	Proper spelling, punctuation, and capitalization used					
10.	Opening captures attention and engages reader					
11.	Compelling thesis presented with a clear road map					
12.	Logically organizes main points with graceful transitions					
13.	Each paragraph well develops one easily identified idea.					
14.	Conclusion summarizes subject or restates thesis and main points.					
	STYLE	Poor 1	Fair 2	Good 3	Very Good 4	Excellent 5
15.	Engaging writer's persona communicates with warmth and passion					
16.	Writer quickly establishes authority and engenders trust.					
17.	Strong verbs and active voice used wherever possible					
18.	Pleasing use of variety in both sentence and paragraph lengths					
19.	Avoids fragments and run-on sentences					
20.	All deadwood removed—no wordiness or *unintended* redundancy					
21.	Emphasizes ideas through intentional repetition & parallel construction					

GLOSSARY

TERMS & DEFINITIONS
GLOSSARY

Note: Words can be viewed in-context in the lesson and on the page indicated in parentheses beside them.

Abdera (7-62)	
agnostic (3-29)	
Agrigento (6-52)	
Akragas (6-52)	
alliteration (4-32, 34)	
allusion (4-32)	
Anaxagoras (6-59)	
Anaximander (1-9)	
Anaximenes (1-9)	

TERMS & DEFINITIONS

anthropomorphic (3-22)	
antithesis (6-60)	
apeiron (1-9)	
aphorism (4-32)	
apologia (7-62)	
Arabia (2-14)	
arche (1-4)	
Archelaus (6-59)	
Aristotle (2-11)	
asceticism (8-72)	

Athens (7-61)	
Aulus Gellius (7-62)	
autonomy (4-31)	
Babylon (1-2)	
Baudhayana (2-16)	
Boyle, Robert (8-79)	
Callicles (7-70)	
Causabon, Isaac (8-79)	
censure (8-72)	
Chaldean (1-2)	

GLOSSARY

TERMS & DEFINITIONS

cliché (4-33)	
Colophon (3-21)	
commune (2-11)	
cosmogony (3-22)	
cosmological (4-34)	
Croton (2-11)	
Cudworth, Ralph (8-79)	
Darwin, Charles (6-51)	
deflect (7-64)	
Delian League (7-64)	

democracy (6-52)	
Democritus (8-71)	
dialectic (5-49)	
dichotomy (8-74)	
Diogenes Laertius (1-1)	
discourse (5-42)	
dropsy (4-36)	
dualism (2-16)	
Elea (3-26)	
elucidation (3-24)	

GLOSSARY

TERMS & DEFINITIONS

Empedocles (6-51)	
empirical (3-29)	
Ephesus (4-31)	
Epicurus (8-79)	
epistemology (3-25)	
equivocation (6-55)	
Etruria / Etruscan (2-18)	
Euripides (4-32)	
extant (2-12)	
extremism (2-11)	

fallacy (5-44)	
foible (8-76)	
formal fallacy (7-65)	
Garibaldi, Giuseppe (6-52)	
garrison (1-4)	
genealogy (3-22)	
geometer (1-2)	
Gorgias (7-62, 69)	
Gymnosophist (8-72)	
gymno (8-72)	

GLOSSARY

Terms & Definitions

Helen of Troy (7-62)	
Heraclitus (4-31)	
Herodotus (1-1)	
Hesiod (1-1)	
hexameter (3-22)	
Homer (1-1)	
hylozoistic (6-59)	
Iamblichus (2-12)	
Iliad (3-22)	
illusory (8-80)	

impiety (7-66)	
incorporeal (1-9)	
informal fallacy (7-65)	
inquiry (5-42)	
Ionian (1-8)	
Ionian League (3-28)	
irreducible complexity (6-55)	
Jones, Jim (2-11)	
Judea (2-14)	
literary device (5-41)	

GLOSSARY

Terms & Definitions

litigious (7-62)	
liturgy (7-62)	
logos (4-31)	
Lydia/Lydian (1-1)	
Magi (8-71)	
Magna Graecia (2-18)	
materialism (2-16)	
Melissus of Samos (5-49)	
metaphor (4-32, 34)	
metaphysics (5-46)	

metempsychosis (2-16)	
Miletus (1-2)	
misappropriate (7-64)	
monism (5-41)	
monist (1-9)	
monotheism (3-26)	
More, Henry (8-79)	
Muse (1-10)	
naturalism (1-6)	
natural selection (6-51)	

GLOSSARY

TERMS & DEFINITIONS

neo (2-12)	
Neobabylonian (1-2)	
Neoplatonist (2-12)	
Newton, Isaac (8-79)	
Nous (6-59)	
Odyssey (3-22)	
oligarchy (6-52)	
omnipotent (3-21)	
omnipresent (3-21)	
omniscient (3-21)	

ontology (5-45)	
ontos (5-45)	
oracle (1-9)	
orator (1-7)	
paradox (5-49)	
Paris (7-62)	
Parmenidean (8-74)	
Parmenides (5-41)	
Parthenon (7-64)	
patrimony (8-72)	

TERMS & DEFINITIONS

Pericles (7-64)	
philia (1-4)	
philosophy (1-4)	
Phoenicia (2-14)	
pithy (4-32)	
Platonist (2-12)	
pluralist (1-9)	
plurality (6-59)	
polis (3-22)	
polytheistic (1-1)	

Porphyry (2-12)	
posit (3-29)	
presupposition (8-72)	
problematic (8-79)	
Protagoras (7-61)	
Protagoras (7-66)	
Pythagoras (2-11)	
Pythia (2-12)	
red herring (7-65)	
reductio ad absurdum (5-49)	

Terms & Definitions

rendezvous (5-41)	
republic (6-52)	
rhetoric (7-64)	
satrap (4-31)	
Seldon, John (8-79)	
sentence fragments (5-43)	
sepulcher (8-72)	
Sextus Empiricus (3-21)	
Sicily (3-26)	
simile (4-32, 33)	

Simplicius (3-21)	
Socrates (4-32)	
Socratic dialogues (5-42)	
sophia (1-4)	
sophist (7-62)	
sophistes (7-69)	
sophos (7-69)	
spontaneous generation (6-55)	
Strabo (8-79)	
syllogism (7-65)	

TERMS & DEFINITIONS

tabula rasa (8-75)	
Temple of Apollo (1-9)	
Temple of Artemis (4-32)	
Thales of Miletus (1-1)	
Theogony (3-22)	
transcendent (1-7)	
traverse (8-73)	
treatise (5-41)	
tyrant (2-14)	
Tyre (2-12)	

unification (6-52)	
University of Strasbourg (6-51)	
Xenophanes (3-21)	
Xenophon (5-42)	
Zeno of Elea (5-49)	

GLOSSARY

TERMS & DEFINITIONS